Where on Earth are Mountains?

Bobbie Kalman

Crabtree Publishing Company

www.crabtreebooks.com

Created by Bobbie Kalman

For Hermine and Barry Steinberg,
our two very talented friends

**Author and
Editor-in-Chief**
Bobbie Kalman

Editor
Kathy Middleton

Proofreader
Crystal Sikkens

Photo research
Bobbie Kalman

Design
Bobbie Kalman
Katherine Berti

Prepress technician
Katherine Berti

Print and production coordinator
Margaret Amy Salter

Illustrations
Robert MacGregor: page 6 (top right)
Vanessa Parson-Robbs: page 28

Photographs
iStockphoto: page 30 (top)
Shutterstock: Jacek Kadaj: page 17 (bottom);
    Meiqianbao: page 14 (bottom)
Thinkstock: pages 9 (top and bottom), 11 (bottom),
    20 (middle right), 23 (bottom right)
Wikimedia Commons: Sergey Prokudin-Gorsky:
    page 12 (bottom); NASA/Michael Studinger:
    page 29 (bottom)
All other images by Shutterstock

Library and Archives Canada Cataloguing in Publication

Kalman, Bobbie, author
        Where on Earth are mountains? / Bobbie Kalman.

(Explore the continents)
Includes index.
Issued in print and electronic formats.
ISBN 978-0-7787-0501-7 (bound).--ISBN 978-0-7787-0505-5 (pbk.).--
ISBN 978-1-4271-8230-2 (pdf).--ISBN 978-1-4271-8226-5 (html)

        1. Mountains--Juvenile literature. I. Title. II. Series: Explore
the continents

GB512.K35 2014   j551.43'2   C2014-900890-2
                                                              C2014-900891-0

Library of Congress Cataloging-in-Publication Data

Kalman, Bobbie.
  Where on earth are mountains? / Bobbie Kalman.
        pages cm. -- (Explore the continents)
  Includes index.
   ISBN 978-0-7787-0501-7 (reinforced library binding : alkaline
paper) -- ISBN 978-0-7787-0505-5 (paperback : alkaline paper) --
ISBN 978-1-4271-8230-2 (electronic-pdf) -- ISBN 978-1-4271-8226-5
(electronic-html)
  1. Mountains--Juvenile literature. I. Title.

  GB512.K354 2014
  910.914'3--dc23
                                                              2014004890

Crabtree Publishing Company
www.crabtreebooks.com   1-800-387-7650

Printed in the USA/052014/SN20140313

Published in Canada
Crabtree Publishing
616 Welland Ave.
St. Catharines, Ontario
L2M 5V6

Published in the United States
Crabtree Publishing
PMB 59051
350 Fifth Avenue, 59th Floor
New York, New York 10118

Published in the United Kingdom
Crabtree Publishing
Maritime House
Basin Road North, Hove
BN41 1WR

Published in Australia
Crabtree Publishing
3 Charles Street
Coburg North
VIC 3058

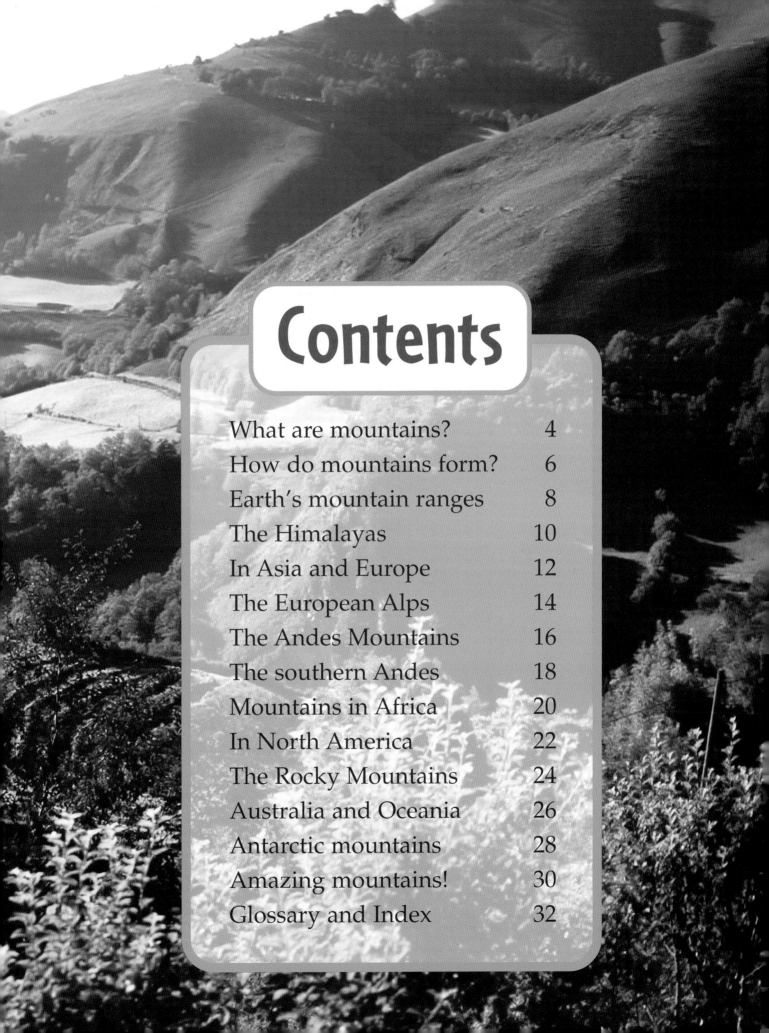

Contents

What are mountains?

Mountains are areas of rocky land that rise high above the ground. They are big, tall, **landforms**. Landforms are different shapes of land on Earth. Mountains cover almost one-quarter of the Earth's surface. They are on every **continent** in the world. The continents are seven huge land areas on Earth. Mountains are also found in **oceans**. Oceans are big bodies of salty water. Find Earth's seven continents and five oceans on the map below.

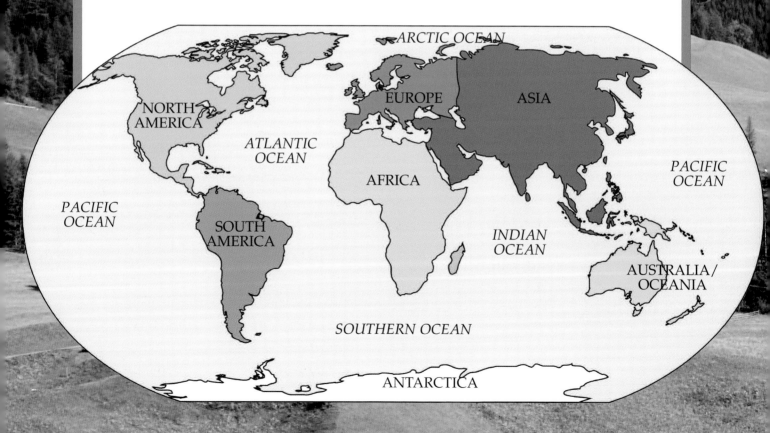

ARCTIC OCEAN

EUROPE

ASIA

NORTH
AMERICA

ATLANTIC
OCEAN

PACIFIC
OCEAN

AFRICA

PACIFIC
OCEAN

SOUTH
AMERICA

INDIAN
OCEAN

AUSTRALIA/
OCEANIA

SOUTHERN OCEAN

ANTARCTICA

peak

tree line

hill

hill

valley

At the top of very high mountains, the weather is cold, dry, and windy. Trees cannot grow there. The **boundary** where trees stop growing is called the **tree line**. Only tough grasses, bushes, and other small plants can survive above the tree line, where there is little soil.

Most mountains have **steep** sides that rise almost straight up from the ground to the **peak**, or top. The peak is narrow and pointed. Hills are short, small mountains with **sloping** sides, which are not very steep. **Valleys** are low areas of land between hills or mountains.

How do mountains form?

Mountains are made of rock. They are different sizes and shapes and are formed in different ways. Mountains are part of Earth's **crust**. The crust is the rocky top layer of Earth. We live on Earth's crust. Under the crust, there is a layer of Earth called the **mantle**. The mantle contains **magma**. Magma is red-hot, melted rock.

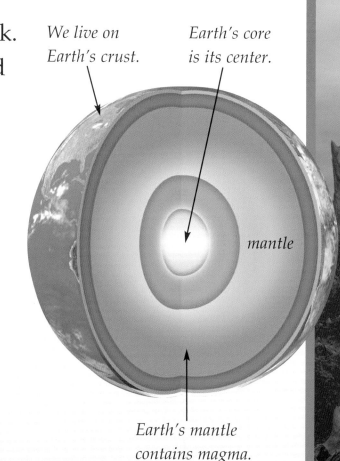

We live on Earth's crust.

Earth's core is its center.

mantle

Earth's mantle contains magma.

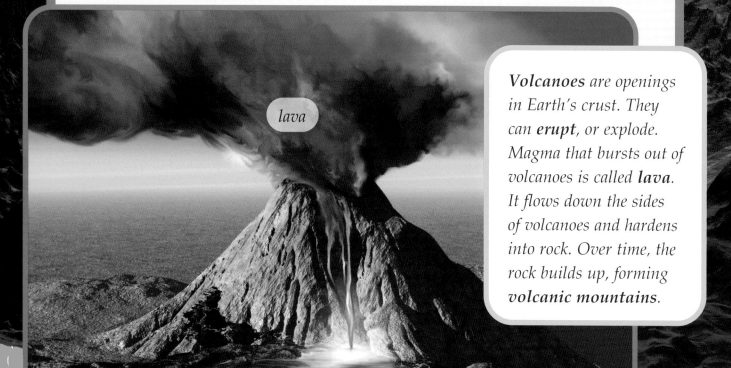

lava

Volcanoes are openings in Earth's crust. They can **erupt**, or explode. Magma that bursts out of volcanoes is called **lava**. It flows down the sides of volcanoes and hardens into rock. Over time, the rock builds up, forming *volcanic mountains*.

Dome mountains *are formed when hot magma rises under the Earth's crust and pushes up the rock above it, forming circular mounds called domes. The Adirondack Mountains in New York State are dome mountains.*

Fault-block mountains *form when Earth's crust cracks, and some of the land along the cracks, or faults, breaks into giant blocks. The blocks that are pushed upward form mountains, such as the Sierra Nevada Mountains in California.*

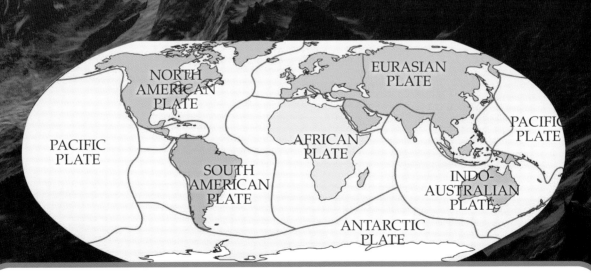

*Earth's crust is made up of **tectonic plates**, or huge pieces of rock. **Fold mountains** are formed when two tectonic plates push together, and the pressure forces the edges of the plates upwards into a series of folds. Most big mountains were formed this way.*

Earth's mountain ranges

Most mountains are part of **mountain ranges**. Mountain ranges are groups of mountains that are close together. There are many mountain ranges on Earth. The Himalayas in Asia form Earth's highest mountain range. The Andes in South America form the world's longest mountain range. The Rocky Mountains, or Rockies, in North America, make up the second-longest range.

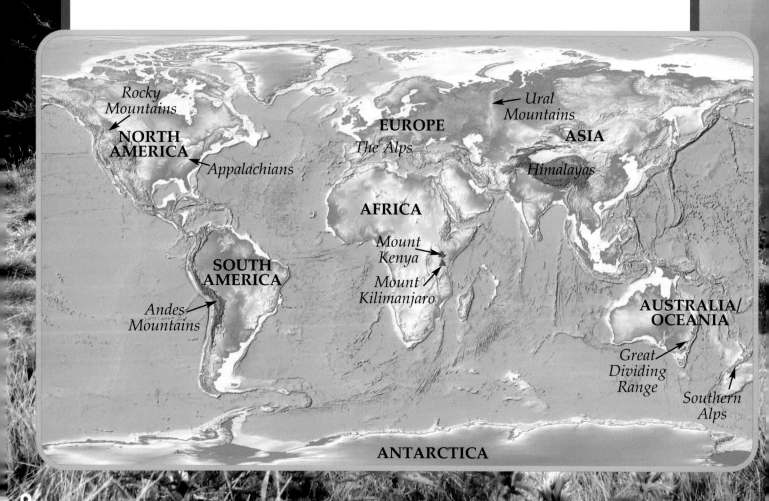

Rocky Mountains

NORTH AMERICA

Appalachians

EUROPE
The Alps

Ural Mountains

ASIA

Himalayas

AFRICA

SOUTH AMERICA

Mount Kenya

Mount Kilimanjaro

Andes Mountains

AUSTRALIA/ OCEANIA

Great Dividing Range

Southern Alps

ANTARCTICA

The Himalayas are the highest mountains in the world. Mount Everest, the tallest mountain on Earth, is part of the Himalayas (see pages 10–11).

The Andes Mountains form the world's longest mountain range. Learn more about these mountains on pages 16–19.

The Rocky Mountains stretch along the western coast of North America from British Columbia, Canada, to New Mexico in the United States (see pages 24–25).

The Himalayas

Asia is the largest continent on Earth, and the Himalayas are the highest mountains. The Himalayas are located in the southern part of Asia and extend across more than 1,500 miles (2,414 km). They touch or cross six countries: Bhutan, India, Nepal, China, Afghanistan, and Pakistan. Mount Everest is the tallest mountain in the Himalayas. Its peak is 29,029 feet (8,848 m) tall.

The thick fur coats and short ears of the snow leopard help these cats keep warm during the cold Himalayan winters.

yak

Yaks are well adapted to high mountains. They have large lungs and hearts to help them breathe, a layer of fat that keeps them warm, and hoofs that help them climb high mountains.

*Red pandas live in trees in the forests of the Himalayas and in southwestern China. They eat **bamboo**, eggs, birds, and berries.*

Mount Everest

Earth's plates are always moving

The Himalayas are fold mountains that were created as the edges of Earth's crust pushed up against one another. Today, plates in the Earth's crust are still moving, causing small **earthquakes** in the Himalayas. In 2005, however, a huge earthquake in Pakistan killed 75,000 people.

People come from all over the world to climb Mount Everest. These climbers are preparing equipment before they start their climb up Mount Everest in Nepal.

In Asia and Europe

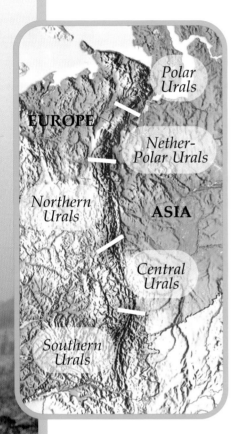

The Ural Mountains run through western Russia, splitting the country into the continents of Europe and Asia. The Urals are divided, from north to south, into the Polar, Nether-Polar, Northern, Central, and Southern Urals. The Urals are rich in **minerals** and have been a major source of **industry** for Russia. Many people live in the cities of the Central and Southern Urals and work in the factories there.

*The Ural Mountains contain about 48 kinds of valuable minerals. For many years, people have worked **mining**, or digging these minerals out of rock. In 1910, a family with shovels and horse-drawn carts is working at the iron mines in the Southern Urals.*

Cold and windy

The Northern Urals have bitterly cold winters. The area at the base of the mountains is called the **tundra**. On the tundra, the ground under the soil is always frozen, so only short plants are able to grow there.

Arctic foxes live on the tundra of the Polar Urals. They have thick fur that turns white in winter.

Eurasian brown bears live in the forests that grow on the lower parts of the Ural Mountains.

European polecats live in the forests that grow on the Southern Urals. They eat mice, frogs, and birds.

The European Alps

The Alps span 750 miles (1,200 km) across the continent of Europe, running mainly through Austria, Germany, Italy, Liechtenstein, Switzerland, France, and five other countries. The mountain range is divided into the Western Alps, Eastern Alps, and Central Alps. The tallest mountain peak is Mont Blanc, which is shared by France, Italy, and Switzerland. It rises over 15,780 feet (4,810 m). Like many large mountain ranges, the Alps are fold mountains.

*Chamonix is a village in France, located on the north side of the **summit**, or highest point, of Mont Blanc. The first Winter Olympics was held there in 1924.*

Glaciers are rivers of ice that are pulled down mountains by *gravity*. They move slowly and pull rocks and soil down with them. They carve out hills, valleys, and lakes. This glacier is called the Great Aletsch Glacier, which is part of the Alps in Switzerland.

glacier

Did you know?

The word "alp" means a very high mountain that is covered in snow for five to six months of the year. Learn about some other alps on Earth on page 26.

This family is skiing on the Matterhorn. The Matterhorn is a mountain in the Central Alps, on the border between Switzerland and Italy. It has one of the highest peaks in the Alps.

The Andes Mountains

The Andes Mountains form the longest mountain range on Earth. They stretch north to south for about 5,500 miles (8,852 km) on the western side of South America. They are part of the countries of Peru, Venezuela, Colombia, Ecuador, Bolivia, Chile, and Argentina. The Andes cover almost the full length of the continent. The mountains separate the rest of South America from the Pacific Ocean.

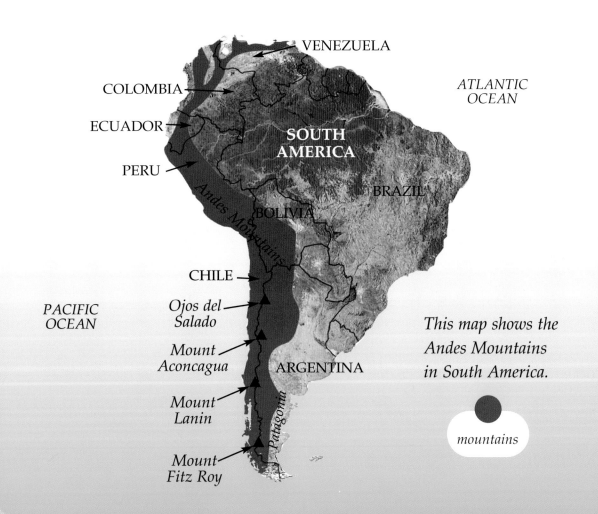

This map shows the Andes Mountains in South America.

● mountains

Machu Picchu in the Andes of Peru was built by the ancient Inca people more than 500 years ago. Thousands of visitors come to see this historic city each year.

These children live in Peru. Their family raises alpacas for their **fiber**, or wool. Alpaca fiber is used for making knitted and woven items, like the clothing worn by these children. Traditional Peruvian designs are woven into blankets, sweaters, hats, gloves, scarves, and skirts.

17

The southern Andes

Mount Aconcagua has the highest peak in the Andes. It is 22,841 feet (6,962 meters) high and is located in Argentina. The mountain has a number of glaciers. Many volcanoes can also be found in the Andes. Ojos del Salado is a massive **stratovolcano** in the Andes on the Argentina–Chile border. It is the highest active volcano in the world. Another volcano in the Andes is Mount Lanin, shown below.

The man on horseback is a **gaucho**, or cowboy. For 300 years, gauchos have traveled on horseback in the **plains** below the Andes Mountains, herding livestock and doing farm chores on huge ranches.

Mount Lanin is one of many volcanoes in the Andes. It lies between Argentina and Chile.

Mount Lanin

Andes

Mount Fitz Roy rises above a plain in the Patagonia region. It has steep granite sides that are hard to climb.

glacier

The Andean fox lives in the southern regions of Patagonia in mountains, deserts, and forests.

Guanacos are wild animals found on high, flat areas in the Andes. They are related to llamas, which are **domesticated** animals.

Mountains in Africa

Mount Kilimanjaro is Africa's highest and the tallest free-standing mountain in the world. It is 19,341 feet (5,895 m) from its base to its summit. Kilimanjaro is composed of three volcanic cones. It is a giant stratovolcano that began forming a million years ago from layers of lava and ash. Mount Kenya, also a stratovolcano, is the second-highest mountain. Other mountains in Africa are shown on the map below.

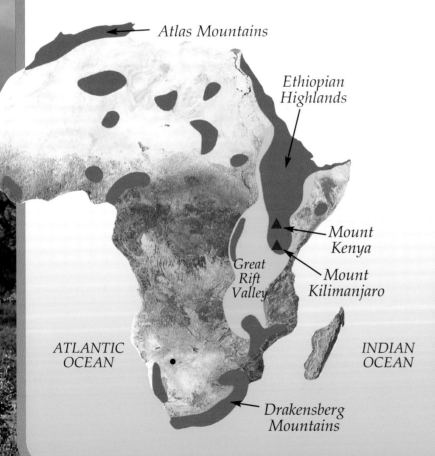

Atlas Mountains

Ethiopian Highlands

Mount Kenya

Great Rift Valley

Mount Kilimanjaro

ATLANTIC OCEAN

INDIAN OCEAN

Drakensberg Mountains

Mount Kenya

The brown areas on this map show some of the mountains in Africa. The bright green area shows the Great Rift Valley, one of the largest valleys in Africa.

Mount Kilimanjaro is in the country of Tanzania, but it can be seen from Kenya, its neighboring country, where this elephant lives. Kilimanjaro is a large stratovolcano with three cones: the Mawenzi and Shira cones are **extinct**, but Kibo, shown here, is **dormant** and could erupt again. It is the highest cone.

Mount Kilimanjaro

In North America

There are 23 **countries** in North America. The largest are Canada, the United States, Greenland, and Mexico. Most of the other countries are islands. North America has many mountains. Mount McKinley, or Denali as it is known to Native peoples, is the highest mountain peak. It is located in the state of Alaska. Mount Logan is the highest mountain in Canada and the second-highest in North America. It is located in the Yukon Territory. Other important mountain ranges in North America are the Appalachians and the Rocky Mountains.

ALASKA YUKON

Denali

Mount Logan

NEWFOUNDLAND AND LABRADOR

ALBERTA

CANADA

BRITISH COLUMBIA

UNITED STATES

PENNSYLVANIA

Rocky Mountains

DENVER

Appalachians

GEORGIA

COLORADO

ALABAMA

PACIFIC OCEAN

NEW MEXICO

MEXICO

ATLANTIC OCEAN

CENTRAL AMERICA

The Appalachians

The Appalachian Mountains are located in the eastern part of North America. They extend almost 2,000 miles (3,218 km), from the Canadian province of Newfoundland and Labrador, to the state of Alabama in the United States. These mountains are among the oldest mountains on Earth. They are divided into three regions: the northern, central, and southern Appalachians. The southern Appalachians have the highest summit, Mount Mitchell. The Blue Ridge Mountain Range, shown here, is part of the southern Appalachians, stretching from Georgia to Pennsylvania.

Mount McKinley, also known as Denali, has a summit of 20,237 feet (6,168 m).

Mount Logan is part of the St. Elias Mountain Range in the Yukon, in northwest Canada.

The Rocky Mountains

The Rocky Mountains are located in the western part of North America. They are more than 3,000 miles (4,828 km) long. They stretch from Alberta and British Columbia in Canada, to New Mexico in the United States. The Rockies are part of the American Cordillera, a chain of mountain ranges that form the western "backbone" of North America, Central America, South America, and Antarctica.

The highest mountains in the Rockies are in Colorado. Many peaks are more than 10,000 feet (3,048 m) tall. This city is Denver, the largest city in Colorado. The Rocky Mountains can be seen behind the city.

This mountain goat and her kid, or baby, have climbed up onto a high peak in the Rocky Mountains. Their hoofs grip the rocks and keep the animals from slipping.

This picture of the Rocky Mountains is taken during the morning sunrise at Moraine Lake in Banff National Park in Alberta, Canada. Forests of **conifers** grow on the low sides of the mountains. Conifers are trees with cones. Their leaves look like needles.

Australia and Oceania

Australia's Great Dividing Range is the third-longest mountain range in the world. It stretches more than 2,175 miles (3,500 km). Mount Kosciuszko, Australia's highest peak, is 7,310 feet (2,228 m). It is in the Snowy Mountains of the Australian Alps, which are part of the Great Dividing Range. On New Zealand's South Island, mountains called Southern Alps can be found. Where else in the world are mountains called Alps located?

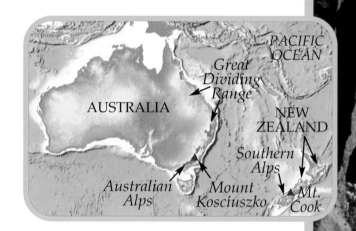

The tallest peak in the Southern Alps is Mount Cook, at 12,316 ft (3,754 m). The Southern Alps contain thousands of glaciers.

Volcanoes can be found all over Oceania, and many are in oceans. When they erupt, they create new land. The islands of Hawaii, which are part of Oceania, are the tops of a great undersea mountain range formed by volcanoes. The volcanoes are still creating land. The mountains shown here are part of the island of Kauai.

The three rocks on this mountain, called the Three Sisters, are in the Blue Mountains National Park, on the eastern part of the Great Dividing Range in Australia. The peaks formed thousands of years ago through erosion.

Antarctic mountains

The highest mountain in Antarctica is Mount Vinson, also known as Vinson Massif. It is 16,066 feet (4,897 m) high. The Transantarctic Mountains, or TAM, which run north and south, form a huge mountain range near the middle of Antarctica. With a total length of about 2,174 miles (3,500 km), the Transantarctic Mountains form among the longest mountain ranges on Earth.

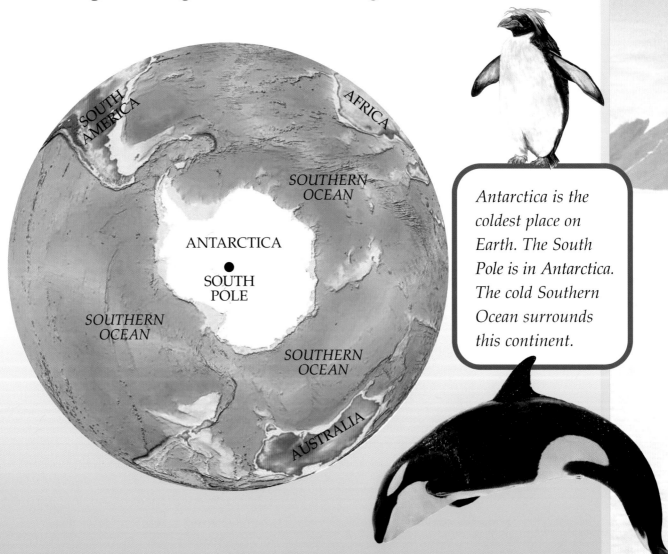

SOUTH AMERICA

AFRICA

SOUTHERN OCEAN

ANTARCTICA

SOUTH POLE

SOUTHERN OCEAN

SOUTHERN OCEAN

AUSTRALIA

Antarctica is the coldest place on Earth. The South Pole is in Antarctica. The cold Southern Ocean surrounds this continent.

ANTARCTIC
PENINSULA

Transantarctic
Mountains

Mount
Vinson

EAST
ANTARCTICA

WEST
ANTARCTICA

Ross
Ice Shelf

The Transantarctic Mountains extend across the continent. They divide East Antarctica and West Antarctica.

Transantarctic Mountains

Mount Vinson is part of the Ellsworth Mountains, shown here.

Amazing mountains!

The mountains in this book are some of the longest and highest, but the mountains on these pages are truly amazing! Which one would you like to visit, climb, or paint a picture of?

Table Mountain is a flat-topped mountain overlooking the city of Cape Town in South Africa. Together with Devil's Peak, Signal Hill, and Lion's Head, the mountains form a natural **amphitheater** around Cape Town's city center.

Devil's Peak

Table Mountain

Lion's Head

Signal Hill

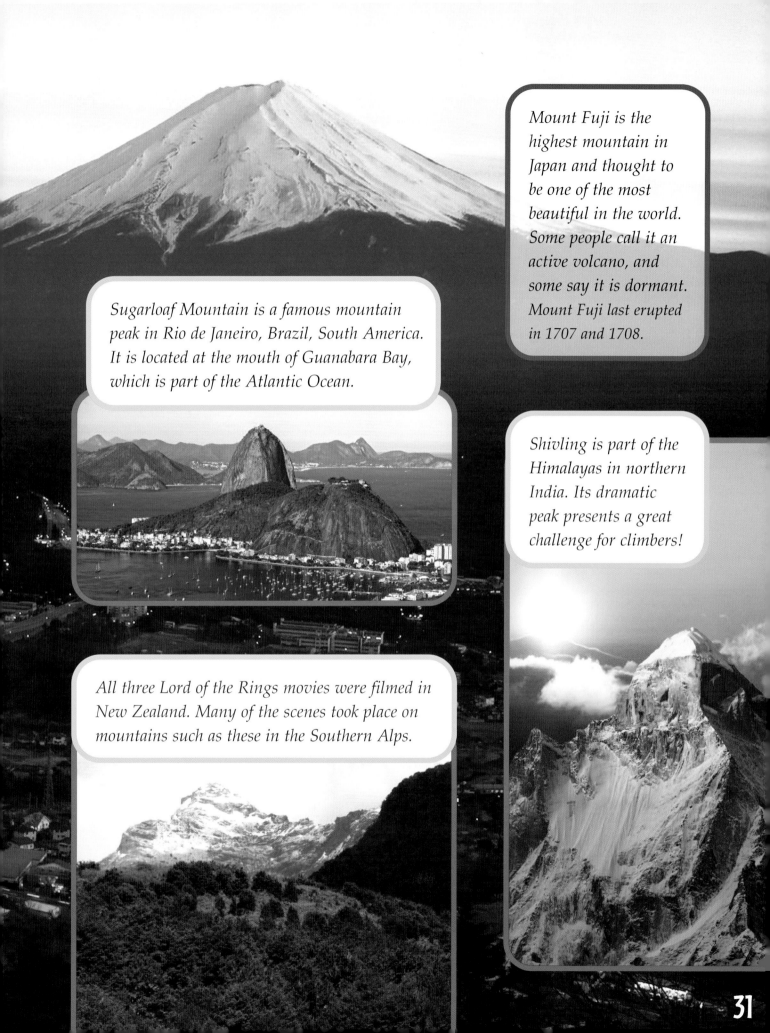

Mount Fuji is the highest mountain in Japan and thought to be one of the most beautiful in the world. Some people call it an active volcano, and some say it is dormant. Mount Fuji last erupted in 1707 and 1708.

Sugarloaf Mountain is a famous mountain peak in Rio de Janeiro, Brazil, South America. It is located at the mouth of Guanabara Bay, which is part of the Atlantic Ocean.

Shivling is part of the Himalayas in northern India. Its dramatic peak presents a great challenge for climbers!

All three Lord of the Rings movies were filmed in New Zealand. Many of the scenes took place on mountains such as these in the Southern Alps.

Glossary

Note: Some boldfaced words are defined where they appear in the book.

amphitheater A semi-circular theater or open area with higher areas around it

bamboo A tall, woody grass that grows in warm areas of the world

boundary Something that separates one thing or area from another

country An area of land with boundaries and borders

dormant A volcano that has not erupted for many years but might erupt again

domesticated Referring to animals that have been raised by people

earthquake A shaking of the ground caused by movements of the Earth's crust or by volcanic action

extinct A volcano that has not erupted for thousands of years

gravity A force that pulls things towards Earth's center

industry Manufacturing or creating something to sell for money

mineral A non-living substance found in nature and obtained by mining

plain A flat area of land with few trees

stratovolcano A volcano that is tall and cone-shaped and which has many layers of hardened lava

Index